ugly.

Ramona J. Ragland

BK Royston Publishing
P. O. Box 4321
Jeffersonville, IN 47131
502-802-5385
http://www.bkroystonpublishing.com
bkroystonpublishing@gmail.com

© Copyright – 2020

All Rights Reserved. No part of this book may be reproduced, stored in a retrieval system, or transmitted by any means without the written permission of the author.

Cover Design Art: Aesthetic Ordonnance and
Ramona J. Ragland
Cover Design Layout: Aesthetic Ordonnance and
Ramona J. Ragland

ISBN-13: 978-1-951941-43-7

Printed in the United States of America

COVER ART

Photography:

Aesthetic Ordonnance

Tiera Owens, Owner

www.aestheticordonnance.com

Makeup:

the locd MUA

Kelli Neché, Owner

Instagram: @thelocdmua

Styling:

Styled by Sadarhi

Sadarhi Cowan, Owner

Instagram: @_darhixo

Hair:

Third Level Style Salon

Kydra Berkeley, Owner

Instagram: @thirdlevelstyle

In loving memory of my grandparents and my beautiful Aunt Pat.

THANK YOU

Thank You, Lord, for Your grace and mercy. It has kept me. Your love saved my life. I am eternally grateful.

To my family, I love you deeply. Thank you for your love and support. Thank you for being there. You inspire me daily. It is an honor to be a Ragland.

To my friends, you all know who you are. You carried me when I couldn't walk. You saw me when I didn't want to be seen. Thank you for your presence. Thank you for your love.

To my ace, my homie, this book came from you. This book would not have been born, or even thought of, without you. You thrust me into purpose...and don't even know it. Thank you...for everything.

To every leader, mentor, teacher who believed in me and prayed for me, thank you. I acknowledge and honor you. This is a fruit of your investment. Thank you.

Love always,

Ramona

DEDICATION

First, I dedicate this book to God. Thank You for Your unconditional love. Thank You for the breath of life. Thank You for Your patience with me. Thank You for this gift. I love You always.

Secondly, this book is dedicated to my parents and grandparents.

Grandma and Grandpa Ragland, you worked so hard for this family. I pray that I honor your name properly in my life. Grandpa Joseph, your daughter raised me well. You'd be so proud. Grandma Rose, I still miss you. I wonder what you would've thought of this. Your smile is so clear to me as I write this.

Mom and Dad, there are not enough words to express my appreciation for you. I pray that this book makes you proud. Thank you for laying the foundation of a legacy upon which I can build. What you have started will last for generations to come. You are exceptional parents and wonderful people. Thank you for loving me. Thank you for being a part of this. Thank you for believing in me. I will honor you for the rest of my days. You are worthy and deserving of every good thing that comes your way. I love you so much.

Love,

Mona

TABLE OF CONTENTS

Thank You	v
Dedication	vii
Foreword	xi
Introduction	xiii
Chapter 1: ugly thoughts.	1
Chapter 2: ugly heart.	15
Chapter 3: ugly habits.	33
Chapter 4: ugly relationships.	55
Chapter 5: ugly beautiful.	77
Conclusion	89
Resources	95
About the Author	97

FOREWORD

For many years, we have told our daughter that she should write a book to add to her many accomplishments. Her talent and writing skills are impeccable. She articulates well and expresses her feelings in relatable ways. We envisioned that she would write some sort of book or novel at some point.

Ramona is someone who enjoys helping people, especially in her community. We raised her to be a caring, giving person, and to help whenever you can. With this book, she plans to help every reader heal and live a fulfilling life. We hope that people will use this book as a tool to help them recognize their faults and "ugliness" and to make changes to better themselves.

In closing, Ramona, we are so proud of you and congratulate you on a job well done. We're glad you finally took our advice! We love you much, and best wishes.

Blessings,
Mom & Dad
XO XO

INTRODUCTION

You are strong. Yes...you. No matter where you are, what you're doing, you are STRONG. You are full of purpose. Let's unlock that!

This book is about purpose. Though we will discuss emotional topics and address matters of the heart, I want you to be reminded that you are a WARRIOR. You have authority and power. You are equipped for ALL that God has called you to accomplish. You are a pioneer and trailblazer. It is my prayer that this book brings out new beliefs about yourself, unknown gifts, and a new understanding of the power that you possess.

This book is for EVERYBODY! I know that many women will read this book. However, this book is for men also. This is not geared towards one or the other. Men, I want you to know that you have a place here also. This book is for you also! You are valuable. *Your healing is important to me, too.* We need you!

Each chapter will include the following:
- Prayer
- Practical application
- A song to encourage and empower us

Throughout the book, you will also find occasional Reflection pages that will give you space to write down what you learn about yourself and what God speaks to you. Keep a pen handy.

Thank you for choosing this book, for trusting my voice. It is my first; and I am elated by your interest and your desire to tap into your strength. This is not as much of an investment in me, as it is in yourself.

This book was born from heartbreak...years of it.

I'm going to say this out the gate - I am not a victim. I am a victor. The above statement is an acknowledgement of my experiences; not a reason to look for pity. We have ALL had our share of heartbreak; ALL of us. Heartbreak is not just relative to romantic relationships. We can have our heart broken by any person or an experience. Heartbreak violently opens your heart and exposes what's inside. It's an involuntary breaking that leaves you vulnerable and in pain. That kind of experience can take years to overcome. But if you intentionally seek healing, and participate actively in the process, it won't take forever. You WILL recover.

My journey has not been pretty (has anybody had a glamorous life story, though?). It's left me with lots of scars, and even some bloody wounds that are still healing. Call me ugly, if you must. But my ugliness is full of purpose; it led me here.

I kept hearing the word "ugly." It came to me in the context of showing the ugly parts of me. One of my fears has been to show the unattractive parts of me. I typically conceal the damaged parts of me. If someone sees that I'm less than "perfect," they see that I'm trash...and leave. This is not referring to the physical part of me (though that can be affected also), but the inside of me. After those experiences, I taught myself to be ashamed and hide.

Through a recent experience, I realized a belief I had about myself - I'm ugly (internally). That's a pretty harsh word. It feels like an assault on somebody. It's always used as an insult. But this made me aware of broken places, insecurities, hidden things within me. Regardless of how they got there, or who did what, I OWN those things now. They are mine to overcome. The same is true for you.

Ugly (n): unpleasant or repulsive; very unattractive to look at; offensive to the sense of beauty; morally revolting; mean; hostile; quarrelsome

Let me clarify. Most of the definitions I found did not surround physical appearance. It was mentioned; but it was interesting that many of the definitions referred to the things we can't see.

So... I'm telling you about it. My wounds. My scars. My bad habits. My ugly. I don't know entirely what I'm doing. This book will probably be a bit messy and flawed. But in this, I pray that you discover the beauty in all of the things that embarrass you. It's not to point fingers or blame, it's to acknowledge and take ownership. In this, I pray that you find that you're perfect the way you are. You're an evolving creature, and your process is spectacular (though sometimes painful). You are exceptional...flaws and all. At the end of this, I want you to embrace every ugly thing and let it empower you. Let these ugly things be what gives you the vision to see the beauty in yourself. We're in this together. So...let's walk.

I want to give you permission to feel. You are allowed to feel what you feel. Your feelings are not evil. They indicate places of pain and where you need to focus on healing. They also indicate places of healing and wholeness that simply need to be maintained. Your feelings are yours. As you read this, if you need to cry...cry. If you realize your anger, and need to scream...scream. If you uncover gratitude in your heart...dance. If your experience is like mine, you'll have a myriad of emotions that will evoke lots of responses. You have the freedom to feel and express yourself with me. I pray that, through this book, I can serve as a safe space for you.

Far too often, we are walking around with broken hearts...and nobody knows. I'm not suggesting you broadcast your issues. Even if just with you, God, and this book...be honest about how you feel. Are you mad at God? Are you disappointed with yourself? Are you hurt? Are you unhappy? Use those dark places as flashlights to expose what is broken in you.

Let me also say this - NOTHING is wrong with you. You're perfect. NOTHING is wrong with you.

When I say that, I'm not implying that you have no room for improvement or that you have arrived. I'm talking about who you are, the core of you. *That* is perfect. Do you have behaviors to fix, things to change, bad habits to break, character flaws to identify? Yes! We all do. But who you are, who you were created to be...NOTHING is wrong with YOU!

Keep in mind, the healing process is WORK. I cannot help you avoid that. But I can help make the work of healing more tolerable and rewarding.

Let's not bury the ugly pieces of us; that causes us to be sick. Some of us are physically sick because of suppressed issues and emotions. We need to express ourselves and share. We will learn wisdom about when and what to share. But let's always be honest with God about what's in our hearts, and be open to what He shows us about ourselves.

This is not meant to capitalize on your weakness or vulnerability. This book is to help you feel, be honest about what you're feeling, how to manage your emotions, and help you to walk the path to victory and purpose.

I am praying for you. It won't always be like this. Embrace all that you are! There is so much beauty in the process and on the other side of your trouble.

The best is YET to come for you! ALL things work together for the good. It is my prayer that you begin to believe that again.

xoxo,

Ramona

CHAPTER 1

ugly thoughts.

What do you think about yourself?

Who are you?

Are your initial answers negative? Are they self-deprecating?

From where did those thoughts come?

Everything begins with a thought.

My answers to these questions have not always been pretty if I'm being honest. I didn't think very well of myself, for so many years. I trained myself to be unworthy because I always thought I was. I presented myself as something less than because I always thought I was. Is that true today? No. Have I arrived? No. However, for most of my life, I was blinded to my value. I didn't understand. In my experience, the same seems true for a lot of people.

Here are some things I've thought about myself:
- I'm an afterthought.
- I'll always be the second choice.
- I'm only valuable when I have something to offer.
- I'm not good enough.
- I'm not worthy of better.
- I'm an embarrassment.

We'll talk more about those things, and how they manifested in my life. We'll also talk about how I am overcoming those false perceptions.

Change how you think about yourself. I know what other people said to you. I know that life has confirmed your own beliefs about yourself. Is what you believe true? Or did it just make sense to believe what you saw about yourself?

When we are born, we are innocent and naturally see the best about everything (including ourselves). At some point, our minds become polluted with lies about our identity. Some of us believe lies about ourselves because we didn't know how to do anything but absorb that information. Some of us didn't have the truth to counter those lies. Some of us were too tired to fight the false idea of ourselves.

Listen. I grew up with two parents who, to this day, speak good things over me. Every day, my father tells me how beautiful I am or how pretty I am. He tells me that I'm smart. My mother always spoke over my intelligence and talent as a writer. I share that to say that you can have favorable circumstances, and still have wrong thinking regarding yourself. Life hits us all, at some point. Pain is real; it's loud. The pain of life comes with loud screams from the heart. The internal beliefs that develop from that pain can drown out the good that you initially knew about yourself.

I'm asking you lots of questions and considering various possibilities because you need to identify the root before proceeding. It all starts with your thoughts. It starts with thought patterns that you have adopted and reinforced.

I need you to be open to two things: 1) You may have a false idea about yourself, and 2) There is a better version of you available.

How you feel is based on your thoughts. Your emotions will be driven by your thoughts about a thing. Your emotions filter responses based on your thoughts.

Example: If I think that someone is going to hurt me, and they resemble anything that looks harmful, I may become scared. That's not a bad thing, in itself. This is just an illustration of how your thoughts will cause you to emotionally respond.

Example: On the other hand, if I consider someone to be safe, and they do something that could be interpreted as harmful, I may not be so quick to become afraid. Why? Because my thought about them is that they are safe; not dangerous.

The same is true about ourselves. It starts with us. It starts with our minds. I'll ask again. What do you think about yourself? That will determine how you feel about yourself, how you speak about yourself, respond to yourself, and how you treat yourself. That will determine how you allow others to treat you.

The root of so many of our issues is directly related to perverted views of ourselves. Before we move onto other components of our lives, we must uproot what affects everything else - lies we believe about ourselves.

PRAYER

You are special. You are unique. You are amazing. There is nobody like you. That is an advantage. You are worthy of the best. You deserve good things. Who you are is likable. You are lovable. What you say is important. Your voice is valuable. You are chosen, accepted, and claimed by God! Let me apologize to you. Often, what we believe about ourselves came from another's opinion of us or a lie that was spoken over us. Many of us didn't have a choice regarding the first identity that we received. Many were defenseless in being attached to an untrue identity. Some people may not have even realized that they did that. If this doesn't apply to you, that's okay. But I want to apologize to those who feel like they inherited an identity that was damaging. I want to apologize to those who feel like they had no say regarding their identity. I am sorry if you were clothed with thoughts and opinions about yourself that countered who God created you to be. It is my prayer, that if you have people to forgive, that you do so today. If you must forgive yourself, do that today. Forgiveness is a process. It's not a one and done. However, you can start the process today. Surrender yourself to the process of healing today. You've been hurting long enough. It's time to be free. You will take ownership and control of your life. You have the power to be whole! You will be whole! God will restore you and redeem every tear that you have shed. Your mind is renewed in Christ. He will reveal who He created you to be. You will be sure of your identity. You've been weeping long enough. Joy is coming!

It is so, in Jesus' name. Amen.

PRACTICAL APPLICATION

Connect with God. If you aren't sure how to do this, simply sit alone and say that to Him.

Example: God, I don't know You. I'm not sure how to connect with You. I'm hurt and want to discover who I am. Show me who You are so that I can learn who I am.

Ask yourself the following questions:

- How do you feel about yourself?
- Why do you feel that way about yourself?
- Is your opinion of yourself accurate? Why or why not?
- Who do you want to be?

- What is the root of your negative self-image?

Be honest with yourself. I recommend documenting your answers. You can write them in a journal (physical or digital) or record an audio message for yourself. They'll serve as testimonies of your growth and help you to be accountable for the journey.

Forgive anyone who may have violated your identity.

Forgive yourself for violating your own identity.

Receive the identity that God has given you.

SONGS

"Identity" by Israel & New Breed

"I Know Who I Am" by Israel & New Breed

REFLECTION

_____
_____
_____
_____
_____
_____
_____
_____
_____
_____
_____
_____
_____
_____
_____
_____
_____
_____
_____
_____
_____
_____
_____
_____

CHAPTER 2

ugly heart.

It was a late Sunday night. Emotionally, I was in pain. Tears streamed down my face for hours. My heart was hurting. The last few weeks were hard. It felt like there was nothing I could do about it. I felt so hopeless, broken, unwanted, discouraged. I knew the truth. However, my feelings didn't match what I knew.

The truth is that I'm loved and wanted. There's so much to look forward to. That's not how I felt, though. It felt like the end; and I was devastated.

It always hurts when you experience the tension of what you know versus what you feel.

You can know the truth and still hurt. Your thoughts can be true and healthy, and you can still hurt. That's tough. There's tension in that moment.

The heart is defined as the central or innermost part of something; personality, disposition; the emotional or moral nature as distinguished from the intellectual nature; one's innermost character, feelings, or inclinations.

There is a root in the heart of people that I think is destroying lives. I'm going to focus on that root, so we can demolish its power over you.

Rejection.

Before we dive in, let me warn you. You may be triggered by this chapter. We're gonna get a bit deep in this one. But sit with this and take your time with this information. Don't rush through this chapter. If this chapter makes you feel anxious or upset, there is probably a wound that needs healing. Let it be touched. Let it heal. If it becomes overwhelming to you, pause and pray. God will help you through this.

I believe that almost every issue known to mankind comes from an issue of rejection. This is not based on any scientific evidence or official case study. This comes from my experience with people. I have seen rejection take over people's lives and create such sadness and bitterness and hard hearts. I believe that everything from crime rates to mental health issues would be decreased if rejection didn't have such a hold on people's hearts.

To be rejected is to be one who has not received acceptance or approval. It is to be dismissed as inadequate, inappropriate, or not to one's taste. To be rejected is like being thrown away.

Have you ever felt like that?

I have. It is devastating. It can create a heart-wrenching pain that can physically affect you. The effects of feeling unwanted or disregarded are unpleasant. You can literally feel like you want to die. There is no worse feeling than feeling unwanted and thrown away. In the next chapter, we'll talk about coping with matters of the heart like this.

For now, I'm going to dissect three components of rejection and outline the tendencies of wounded people.

The Seed of Rejection

Rejection is a real experience. It is a real thing. Rejection has done a lot of damage in my own life; so I understand it very well. I can identify it from a mile away. I'm certainly not going to discount anyone's experience. However, we have to change our minds about ourselves. We must be convinced of our own value and worth. It's necessary. When our minds are strong in conviction about who God created us to be, our lives don't fall apart when someone doesn't want us. When we know that we are fearfully and wonderfully made, we aren't as bothered if someone thinks we are trash. When we know that our Father, the God of the universe, loves us unconditionally, we don't die when someone decides they don't love us anymore. When we know that we were hand-crafted by God, we don't hurt as much when we are misunderstood. When we know that God holds our future in His hands, we don't get discouraged when an employer denies us. I believe that rejection has been given so much power in our lives because we're unfamiliar with and unconvinced of the truth about ourselves.

The seed of rejection is the first thought that had permission to establish an illegitimate identity of yourself. It is the initial thought (that can come from multiple sources) that says you're not worth preserving, protecting, loving, or keeping.

Rejection's goal is to confuse your identity, making you feel less than. It affects every area of our lives. It desires to create unhealthy and destructive cycles in your life, based on the false premise that you will always be nothing. It causes depression, suicide, isolation, mental torment, insomnia, addiction, among other things.

The seed of rejection starts in your mind. Most people experience rejection as children, when they may not have yet developed an understanding of who they are.

They're vulnerable, and a bit defenseless when rejection comes lurking around.

It can come from a negative statement, such as:

- You're stupid.
- I never wanted you.
- You're not (insert adjective) enough.
- Why aren't you like "so and so"?
- You never get it right.

It can come from experiences, such as:

- Not being chosen for group projects
- Going through a breakup (in any relationship, not just romantic)
- Being denied a job or promotion
- Feeling misunderstood
- Being abandoned by family

The Reality of Rejection

At some point in our lives, we come into agreement with rejection. Again, it's not that rejection is not a real experience. It is. However, we have the power to reject the idea that we're thrown away. Only trash and unusable things are thrown away. Neither applies to you. You are a treasure and have so much purpose!

In the last chapter, we talked about our thoughts. Our thoughts determine how we feel. Our emotions are based on the opinions and beliefs that we have.

We respond based on our beliefs.

Here are a few realities about rejection:

- Rejection can be subtle. It can come through tone and body language.
- Rejection can be communicated through decisions. It's not always a loud announcement.
- People can reject things they want. If someone doesn't feel worthy of a good thing, they will often push it away (even if they actually want it).
- Rejection has nothing to do with you. If you have been rejected, it's projected insecurity or deficiency from another person. When a person rejects you, they are typically communicating something about themselves that has nothing to do with you. You're just the recipient of their issue.

The Illusion of Rejection

Sometimes, we categorize things as rejection that aren't. The reality is that relationships, friendships, any union (of any degree) with people involve at least two parties. Often, we only focus on our own point of view. If someone isn't there or needs some space, we automatically categorize that as rejection. If someone has to move on, for whatever reason, we feel rejected. I think that's because, naturally, we're prone to feeling rejected. I also think that we mentally prepare ourselves to be rejected. Some people and things are seasonal. We cannot attach ourselves forever, when some things are meant to be temporary. I also think that a lack of understanding of our life season can make a season change feel like rejection. Rejection's goal is to always make you feel insufficient and less than. It will sometimes use real experiences or it will create a false narrative to paint the illusion that you've been rejected. When your mind is sure of who you are, you can discern the difference. Not everyone who leaves or exits is tossing you to the side. Sometimes, a person's exit is for your protection. An exit or distance can come from a place of love. Rejection does not come from a place of love.

Let's remember to give other people grace. Some people really love you; they just have other things to manage.

Tendencies of Wounded People

Rejected people are wounded people. Here are a few things about wounded people that we'll expound on later:

- Hurt people reject people; don't let others in.
- Hurt people prepare to reject others; set people up for failure.
- Hurt people seek validation.
- Hurt people tend to be victims (always blaming everyone else, never taking accountability).
- Hurt people self-sabotage.

Does any of this sound familiar? If it does, have hope. Rejection can be overcome. Hurt can be overcome.

Your wounds can be healed. Your heart will be changed, when you change your mind about yourself.

PRAYER

Rejection has no power in your life. It does not have authority over you. You are not rejected. You are enough. You are not trash. You are not a mistake. You are not an embarrassment. You are not second place. You are not an afterthought. You are important. You are worthy. You are valuable. You are perfectly created. There is NOTHING wrong with you. If someone did not realize or understand your value, that does not reduce your value. Your value is undeniable. I pray that you are healed of all remnants of rejection. You will begin to understand the root of rejection and how it has grown in your life. You will not only identify it, but you will uproot it and heal with God's help. May you begin to discern the difference between real rejection and perceived rejection. Your heart will be open to the love of the Father. You are chosen, accepted, and claimed by God! Never again will you be persuaded to believe that you are anything less than the wonderful being God created you to be.

All of these things are so, in the name of Jesus. Amen.

PRACTICAL APPLICATION

Connect with God. He knows our hearts better than we ever will. He sees the hidden and unknown things in our hearts. Ask Him the following questions:

- Who do I feel rejected by?
- Who actually rejected me?
- When have I felt rejected?
- Why do I feel rejected?
- Have I rejected myself?

Ask God to help you see yourself the way He sees you.

Confess the truth about yourself (see the above prayer). Speak life over yourself. Be kind to yourself.

Forgive anyone or anything that made you feel rejected.

Forgive yourself for giving rejection so much power in your life.

SONG

"Cycles" by Jonathan McReynolds

CHAPTER 3

ugly habits.

The pain was overwhelming. I thought this year was going to be different. After years of going through so much, I thought everything would turn around. Next thing I know...another heartbreak. I felt so defeated, and couldn't be consoled. The same pain that hurt me became my consolation. The sadness became my place of comfort; and I dwelled there. My life became one ball of grief. That grief grew to daily despair. I had more bad days than good. It was so hard. It felt like this was what my life was going to be. It felt like nothing I did got rid of the pain. There were temporary fixes; nothing worked. The pain always came back. My heart was always being broken. I was always messing up. I couldn't move past this place. I was stuck in pain. I lowered my head and accepted what I expected life to be...a lifetime of tears.

Heartbreak hurts.

What do you do when your heart is broken? How do you deal?

Let me reiterate. Heartbreak is not exclusive to romance. It is any scenario where you experienced some sort of disappointment or loss. It is where your heart was torn from a person or thing that you loved (for a variety of reasons). Now, you're left to deal with the remaining contents of your heart. How do you deal with *that*?

If we're honest, many of us don't handle that well. Most people run to unhealthy or destructive things to make us feel better. It's not until after we've gotten tired of the effects of those vices that we decide to heal in healthy ways. It is my prayer that we lead our healing process with healthy coping methods instead of delaying our wellness with toxic habits.

UNHEALTHY COPING

I don't know anyone that enjoys emotional pain. If you know someone who does, that person is a liar. No one wants to walk around in distress. No one. People learn how to deal with it. But no one likes it. We all want to be happy. We all enjoy laughing and smiling. But many people tend to run from pain or suppress it. Is that you? It has certainly been me. At one point,

I referred to myself as the "Queen of Suppression." I am a queen; however, that's not the type of queen I'm trying to be. I'm a different kind of woman today (we'll talk about that later). Most people avoid and pretend like they're not hurting. But that doesn't eliminate the hurt; it just creates the illusion that it's gone. The wound is still very open, whether you acknowledge it or not. Not dealing with it puts you in a cycle of being the victim. The victim mentality always blames others for any negative thing in life; there is never any ownership. Guess what. Whether you are the cause of the pain in your life or not, you are responsible for your healing.

When you're hurting, where do you run? Listed are some vices that we use when we don't want to deal with our afflictions.

How do you cope with issues of the heart? As you read through this list of vices, be honest with yourself. There is no guilt or shame with how you have chosen to cope. Be honest. That's where the healing begins.

Honestly, I could probably write separate chapters on each of these things. Maybe I'll do that in another book. Which one of these applies to you? I have used almost all of these things to make me feel better, to escape the pain of life. Let me tell you what...none of them worked. I was able to feel okay and suppress for short periods of time. But I always hurt again. These vices are not cures. They are things that can destroy your life because you don't want to deal with your heart. Let's walk through each one, briefly, to highlight the danger of using these as emotional medicine.

Alcohol

This one is a favorite of so many people. I think that's because it's so culturally acceptable. Think about it. How many people say they're going to have a drink to relax after a long day at work (raises hand)? How many people say they just wanna have a good time and have a few drinks (raises hand)? How many people say that they just need to get their mind off of things with a few beverages (raises hand)? We have heard all of these things, and more. Whether you agree with alcohol consumption or not, people are running to it to stop the emotional bleeding. The reality is that it causes more bleeding. Your denial gives your wound time and room to grow. Alcohol skews your thinking. Lots of people make calls and texts and visits that they didn't plan to make because of alcohol. Alcohol can damage your liver, increase your risk for cancer, cause weight gain, give you skin problems, allow you to be more depressed, and can lead to death. When you sober up, guess what. The pain is still there. This doesn't work. Before this vice, you just had pain to deal with. Now, you have pain plus the possibility of other health and mental issues.

Drugs

This includes legal and illegal substances. This includes marijuana, meth, heroin, and prescription pills. People use drugs for the same reasons they use alcohol. The difference is that alcohol is a depressant (slowing down the brain). Not all drugs work that way. Some drugs are stimulants (also known as "uppers"), which increase energy. Many of these drugs are very dangerous. They can result in memory loss, dental issues, skin issues, increased heart rate, hallucinations, possible overdoses, and even death. This is damaging to your life. This doesn't work, either.

Sex

I never understood how people ran to sex after heartbreak. It didn't make sense to me...until I had mine broken. Granted, this was not my coping mechanism of choice. But I know people who have chosen it. Part of what this does is make you feel like you've gotten over someone by engaging with a new lover. It creates the illusion that you have power and control. The reality is that this compounds the issue. When you are sexually intimate with someone, you are attaching yourself to that person. I know that some believe that you can have "no strings attached" sex. Maybe in the natural world, you can. But I do believe there is a mental, spiritual, and even emotional attachment that is formed when you have sex with someone; even if it's someone you're not romantically interested in. If you were emotionally broken before sex, guess what. You'll still be emotionally broken afterwards. The difference is that, now, you're tied to someone new. That has complicated your pain. Not only that, there are other risks, such as STDs and pregnancy. This doesn't work, either.

Food

Ahh. Comfort food. We always find a reason to eat, don't we (raises hand)? I enjoy crushing a good meal. Don't we all? There's nothing wrong with enjoying food and smashing a tasty plate. Some of y'all are salivating right now, thinking about what you're gonna eat next. Don't misunderstand my point here. However, some of us have run to food like a drug. Food can be used to stuff emotions that we don't want to deal with. This doesn't just apply to those who binge but also to those who stop eating. I've been on both sides of that coin. Overeating the wrong things can lead to health conditions such as diabetes, obesity, high cholesterol, high blood pressure, and even heart disease. Starving yourself can lead to dehydration, fatigue, bone loss, mood swings, and negative effects on the brain. Not only is the pain still there, now we have another relationship to fix - our relationship with food. This doesn't work.

Shopping

Listen. Who doesn't love a new outfit? A new pair of shoes? A new piece of jewelry? Most of us love retail therapy. I have done, and witnessed, this method of coping. It's fun for a moment. But when your bank account is low, and you have a house full of stuff, you set yourself back. You received momentary relief. But now you have more clutter, less money, and the same pain you came with. This does not work.

Isolation

Man. This one. This one is personal for me. My closest friends are probably giving me an entire side eye with the mention of isolation. They are probably shouting "Amen!" from the rooftops. Anyone who knows me intimately knows that is one of my predominant coping mechanisms. When I am *really* going through, I tend to quietly close doors on people and run away. My squad has given me much feedback about this. This is so unhealthy, y'all. We are meant to do life *with* people. When you are alone, without anyone, it reinforces the perception you have developed about people via pain. It leaves you alone with your thoughts, which tend to replay themselves. You can go a bit crazy trying to get through life alone. It is depressing and not conducive to healing. The reality is that sometimes you need someone to hear you scream, someone to wipe your tears, someone to hold your hand, someone to hug you. Sometimes, you just need someone to be there, even if you don't want to talk about it. We all need safe places. Lean on those people. The people that are meant to be there for you won't count you as a burden; they want to lighten your load. People want to love you. They want to support you. Let them. When you isolate yourself from people you say you trust, you hurt them. By trying to protect them from your damage, you damage them. Isolating yourself will leave you alone and hurting. It can destroy good relationships because you refuse to participate because you won't open up. You have two choices: Hurt alone or hurt with someone. Life is a bit easier when we have someone who can help shoulder our burdens. This is a destructive tendency, and it doesn't work.

Do you notice anything about these unhealthy methods? They all steal from you! The truth is, they can all lead to death! They magnify the pain you came with. You're left with bad health, less money, more clutter, and compounded issues. Don't be deceived by the temporary relief. You *will* pay for the instant gratification, in the long run.

Though these vices seem like effective tools, in the moment, they are all destructive. They will all leave you with the pain you came with, plus more. The pain may intensify and compound because these potential addictions have left you with more issues than when you started.

If you are suffering from addiction, be encouraged. There is hope! You can overcome it. At the end of this book, I will provide helpful resources.

HEALTHY COPING

There are healthy ways to deal with the pain of life. There are productive ways to overcome hurtful moments in life.

Here are some things you can do to start the healing process:

- Acknowledge your feelings. Be honest. That is critical.

- Your feelings are important. However, they should not be leading you entirely. If you feel a specific way, say so; but don't live there. Don't dwell in your emotions.

- Communicate. Some of what you feel may be based on illusion. Conversations can bring so much clarity and healing.

- Go to therapy! This was easily one of the best decisions of my life. A therapist is a professional. They are unbiased and have an objective view of you. They can provide feedback and tools that will help you grow. Going to therapy does not indicate that anything is "wrong" with you. As a matter of fact, it takes courage to admit that you need help in either maintaining something or repairing something. That takes great strength! Therapy will change your life. Please find a therapist. At the end of this book, I'm going to recommend you to an exceptional professional.

Instead of indulging in unhealthy habits, here are some healthy habits to build that you can do to be productive during your process:

- Pray
- Exercise
- Write/journal
- Challenge yourself at work

- Meet new people or reconnect with old friends
- Have fun
- Do new things
- Finish projects that you've been putting off
- Read a book
- Dream!

These things will help you to process your pain in healthy ways! Not only that, they will push you forward mentally, physically, spiritually, emotionally. These things will propel you to a place of healing and wholeness.

PRAYER

God wants you healthy and well. He cares about you. He cares about your well-being. I speak healing and wholeness over you. You are not deficient. Who you are is enough. I break the power of addiction over anyone who is struggling to cope. I speak against confusion and depression in your life. Lord, send the right people into their lives to comfort them. You are near to the brokenhearted. Heal every hurting heart. Draw near to those who are drawing near to You right now. Hear the cries of Your children. You are a Father who cares about every detail of His children's lives. Comfort those who feel lonely. Encourage those who feel hopeless. Wrap Your arms around everyone who is going through a tough emotional season. It is temporary. You will help them. You are walking with them. Hope is being restored right now.

I speak these things, in Jesus' name. Amen.

APPLICATION

- Connect with God. He cares for you. He wants you to enjoy this life; not grieve it.
- Confide in a trusted friend.
- Find a therapist.

SONG

"Smile" by Kirk Franklin

REFLECTION

_____
_____
_____
_____
_____
_____
_____
_____
_____
_____
_____
_____
_____
_____
_____
_____
_____
_____
_____
_____

CHAPTER 4

ugly relationships.

It felt like everybody always left. No one could be trusted. It was like there was an expiration date on people's love for me. Since people left me anyway, I just made it easy for them. That way, I would minimize my heartbreak. I was a vault; almost impossible to open. Yet, a part of me was screaming to share with people. But because I was afraid, I kept myself to myself in relationships. It's like the friend or person I was with became an accessory to a relationship with myself.

First, I'll outline a hierarchy of relationships to help you move forward in healthy relationships. Then, I'm going to talk about the tendencies of damaged people in relationships.

Again, relationships are not just romantic. When I use that word, I'm referring to any connection to another person (friend, boyfriend/girlfriend, fiancée, spouse, acquaintance, associate, etc). However, these things typically show up most with people who are close enough to hurt you.

RELATIONSHIP WITH GOD

God is not like people. God is love. There is no love without Him. This relationship will drive every other relationship in your life. If this one is wrong, you will struggle with other people.

RELATIONSHIP WITH YOURSELF

Your relationship with yourself is based on your relationship with God. Love comes from Him. You must, first, receive love from Him in order to give it to yourself. He defines love. Without that, we create our own version of love and impose it on ourselves and others. If you do not love yourself as you should, revisit your relationship with God. Do you know Him? Do you know that He loves you? Do you know that He cares? Do you believe that?

RELATIONSHIP WITH OTHERS

Your relationships with people, romantic or otherwise, is directly related to your relationship with yourself. You cannot give what you do not have. If you do not love or care for yourself, there is a limit to the quality of love that you can give others. If you have a broken relationship with yourself, please expect that you will create or enter broken relationships with others.

DYSFUNCTION

In this section, we're really going to start to own our "ugly." That honesty is what's going to reveal the best in you. Ownership removes the damage from your life and leaves you with a pure heart. Pastor Dharius Daniels said something profound in his Heart Attack sermon series: "You are not responsible for your hurt. But you are responsible for your healing. They are not coming back to fix you. If you focus on recovery, God will do His part in restoration." Though someone else may have afflicted us, we own the healing. We will not be victims and put our responsibility to heal in anyone else's hands. Don't be scared. I'll share my mess first. You don't judge me. I won't judge you. Deal? Deal.

Love always leaves. This was my mantra for years. I *lived* by this. Obviously, this concept came from real-life experiences. Every time I thought I found someone I could trust, or someone that I could love, it didn't last. For multiple reasons, relationships end. They just do. But because I dealt with rejection since childhood, I saw through the lens of rejection as an adult. Anytime someone didn't stick around, I was terribly hurt. In addition to that, I love intensely and deeply. That made detachment more difficult for me.

So, I had a filtering process and defense mechanism. Perfection. Let me preface this next part with a disclaimer: At the time, I did not realize my behavior. I didn't realize until I grew and evaluated myself in relationships (which I'm still doing). Because I experienced rejection so much in my life, it became an expectation in relationships. Unconsciously, I had impossible standards for people to live up to. That way, when they left, it wasn't surprising. That allowed me to expect a departure. Though it still hurt, I could protect my heart from being as damaged. Nobody is perfect; yet, I expected perfection from people knowing they wouldn't reach that standard. Shoot! I don't even meet that standard. Isn't that crazy? It sounds ridiculous as I articulate it today. But these are the kinds of things that unhealed people do. When you don't pursue healing, the hurt festers and you tend to the desire to hurt other people. Since you won't deal with your own heart's cries, you'll inflict pain somewhere else to distract you from your own pain. In addition to that, pain allows hurt people to bond. That is a trauma bond, and entirely unhealthy. There's a difference between having a traumatic experience in common and becoming intertwined with someone through trauma.

I was afraid to open up to people who were deserving of me. Suppressing feelings and being quiet was something I was great at. Am I an expert in this area now? No...not at all. I actually just found my voice and am learning to speak up and express myself. But I found it to be an act of love to be quiet and not disrupt anyone's life with my feelings. I felt like it was a violation of love by opening up about my feelings, especially if it would possibly upset someone. Today, I understand that it is love that makes room for me to be open with the ones I love the most. Real love is safe.

Let's talk about one last issue. For many years, I believed that in order for someone to love me, I needed something to give. This is performance-based love. Can I be honest? This is something I'm still overcoming. People that love you, love *you*! They don't love you because of what you bring or do, they love *you*! I found myself in relationships where I was always doing so much, no matter the cost. When I didn't, I felt guilty. When I wanted to say "no," I felt awful. Let me also add this - I'm a giver by nature; a very generous one. I've been that way my whole life. Giving is what I do. Serving people I love is just what I do. It brings me joy. However, that characteristic must be managed. When you take a person wired like that and combine it with the belief that love must be earned, it can lead you to dangerous waters. Granted, I wasn't thinking about it. I wasn't thinking, "I need to do xyz so someone will love me or stick around." That wasn't my thought process. However, my actions reflected an unconscious belief that it was necessary to do that. It was like I had to go above and beyond to prove my love for someone; as though my love wasn't enough on its own. See those two issues? 1) I felt like I had to perform for people to love me; 2) I felt like my love wasn't good enough. I overcompensated because of previous hurts. I liked to be needed...because historically I always was needed by someone. How do I function in a relationship where someone doesn't need something from me; they just want *me*? That's a form of codependency, by the way. Here are some negative effects of that: It can make people feel uncomfortable. You take on roles in people's lives that they didn't give you. You can come across as a caretaker instead of a friend. You take people's opportunity to participate in the relationship. You don't give them a chance to do things for you because you're always doing for them. You potentially set yourself up as a god in their lives by always doing everything for them. You are not anybody's God.

Looking back, I realize that I expected people to be God. If they couldn't give what I needed (which should've come from Him), I felt rejected. Listen. I had *real* experiences where I was truly rejected. However, my tendencies came from unresolved pain from those experiences. It also highlights how important it was for me to have a relationship with God. We all have a natural desire to be close to God. He is our Father and Creator. When we try to fill His role in our lives with people, we will always be disappointed. He is the ONLY one who knows me entirely and my whole life from front to back. He never sleeps nor slumbers. He is the ONLY one who is available to me 24/7; the ONLY one.

These things made it so hard for me to receive love. When people truly loved me, it was hard to believe. I have amazing people in my life. I am loved. However, I still have to make sure that I connect with that fact. I still have to consciously allow myself to be loved because I know how far away I used to push love. Isn't it funny that the very things we want the most, we push away? That's the power of fear. Fear will keep you from some wonderful experiences. It will keep you bound in the pain of yesterday.

If you continue with these types of behaviors, eventually people *will* leave. You may end up by yourself. People want safe, trustworthy, and healthy relationships. No one wants to walk on eggshells and pull on you while you give nothing in return, simply to protect yourself. You cannot ask someone else to absorb the entire risk of a relationship while you are fully protected by your defenses. That's not fair to the other person. That hurts them. If someone has committed to opening themselves up to you and inviting you into their lives, you should do the same. Otherwise, you're hurting people the same way others hurt you.

Constantly focusing on your pain, without considering others, is selfish. It will cause you to believe that the world owes you something and should revolve around you. In your mind, that will serve as compensation for all of the times you were hurt. You will also cause yourself to struggle with commitment issues, pushing things away before they can push you away. In all of your protection and defenses from other people, you'll ultimately reject yourself. When no one else is around, you'll become your own victim. You'll struggle with self-worth and receiving love because you give pain the permission to erode your heart. Get healed!

To be quite honest, after having matured, I realized that it takes so much more energy to obsessively protect yourself like that. It's draining. Should you use wisdom in relationships? Absolutely! But give people a chance. Don't enter a relationship just to continually slam doors in people's faces and keep them out of your heart. Otherwise, be alone.

All of these tendencies were cries for help. They were my heart's way of crying for healing. Because I didn't answer that, it caused me to be dysfunctional in relationships.

These tendencies have one thing in common: FEAR. Perfect love casts out fear. If someone truly loves you, they should be a safe place for you; and you'll have no reason to fear. However, you also have to *choose* to trust the safety.

Here are a few truths that I've had to face:
- Not everything is meant for a lifetime. Stop expecting every single interaction or relationship to develop into a lifelong union. That's just not true for everyone. Some people

are seasonal. That's not a bad thing! It's okay! Are some people meant to be around forever? Sure. But that's not everyone. When you expect forever from seasonal relationships, you'll be devastated. You need to discern which is which and be okay with relational transitions.

- You hurt people, too. I know that we always see ourselves as the victims, and never the villains. But guess what. There are people out there who have been hurt by you, too. Understanding this will make you more compassionate and open-minded when it comes to relationships. It will also cause you to give grace when people mess up because you know that you mess up also.

- Maybe you are the common denominator. As wonderful as I was, maybe my tendencies were exhausting to people. If I found that people were always leaving, maybe I had something to do with it. I had to be open to that possibility. As I've grown, I certainly see how this was true in some situations.

OPEN UP

Open up. Be open to being loved. People want to love you. Don't push away genuine love because you're afraid. Don't make them pay for damage that someone else did to you. How much life are you missing because you're afraid to get hurt? Guess what. We will all get hurt. It may not always be intentional; but it's inevitable. What's important is how you recover and grow from each experience. Heartbreak doesn't have to be your lifestyle; it doesn't. You can be loved and love in healthy ways. There are people that are willing to walk through life with you. But you have to be open to those people and give them a chance. What happens is that we hold our future accountable to our past. We get so used to pain that we resist peace. We are so familiar with bitterness that love becomes foreign. Release yourself. Be free. Not everyone is out to hurt you. Part of the beauty of relationships are the ugly moments. That's where intimacy and bonds are created. Everyone can make it through good times. Real relationships can withstand difficulties and still thrive. *That* is the greatest proof of love; not your defenses. Use wisdom. Love. Be loved.

Stop rejecting love. Stop pushing away what is good for you. You can only push something away for so long before it stays where you pushed it.

Heal. BE LOVED.

PRAYER

I speak healing over every broken area of your life. Your heart will be mended. You will be whole. You will not only begin the healing process; but you will stick to it. You will be committed to this process. Your future depends on your wellness. The next generation depends on your wholeness. God's will is for you to be well! He cares about your relationships. They are important to Him. We are not meant to live this life alone. I pray that you forgive and trust again and love again. May every toxic tendency be discontinued and replaced with healthy habits. I pray that you are connected to people who are honest with you and patient with you in your process. I pray that you are surrounded by people who serve as safe places. I pray that you become well enough to serve as one. Change your mind about yourself. YOU are enough. When you realize that, you will receive all the love that you deserve. You are worthy. You will love well. You will receive love well.

Be healed, in Jesus' name. Amen.

APPLICATION

Journal (whether in a book or an audio message) your tendencies and dysfunctional ways in relationships. Be honest with yourself. Document why you have these habits, and what you will do to be healthier in your interactions with others.

Connect with God during this process. He will reveal deep things in your heart that will be helpful for your understanding.

SONGS

"Teach Me" by Musiq Soulchild

"Love's Still Alright" by Chante Moore

CHAPTER 5

ugly beautiful.

It was a cool Friday evening, just before nightfall. There I was broken, emotionally distressed, and alone. There was no hope for me.

There He was...exhausted, beaten, mocked, spit on.

I sat alone quietly, at the foot of the hill, with tears in my eyes. What you don't know is that I had been exiled...because they found out what I did...and I was cast away. I had nobody to comfort me. While walking up the hill, He looked at me. I was hurting so badly and was tired. I didn't trust Him.

His gaze delved deep into my soul. He saw me. He *saw me*. I had never been seen before. It scared me. I had to snap myself out of it because I knew He couldn't be trusted, either. But I couldn't escape the intrigue. Something was different about Him. I believed whatever I felt from Him, even though I wanted to resist it. I was scared of His sincerity. But there was such assurety in His eyes.

He made it to the top of the hill. I saw Him from a distance. He was harassed and assaulted further. I didn't understand why. He seemed so gentle. It didn't look like He was bothering anyone or deserving of what they were doing to Him.

Then, I saw them lift Him up...and nail Him to a wooden cross. My heart broke. I felt a deep anguish for Him. I didn't know Him; but I could feel Him. He was a good man. Why wasn't anyone protecting Him? I learned...it's so He could protect me.

On the inside, I asked "Why?" He set His eyes upon me, and mouthed to me "For you." I was confused because I wasn't close enough for Him to hear my question. Besides, I didn't speak it out loud. It was like He sensed my confusion. He mouthed it again, "For you." I still didn't understand.

I was a chaotic, ugly mess. It felt like I couldn't get life right. Everything I touched was destroyed. I felt so badly about myself. I wasn't smart enough, black enough, small enough, cool enough. What would a Man like that want with someone like me? Why would He say that He was being punished for me? At times, I wasn't worth a call back, and He's telling me that He's being hurt for *me*? He's dying for *me*? What?

This Man knew that I would disregard Him, dishonor Him, run away from Him, deny Him, be angry with Him, ignore Him. He knew the things that I would do and who I would be. He knew how damaged I was. He knew it better than anybody else. He never identified me by my activities. He could've called me a drunk, a whore, a liar, a lazy bum, an emotional wreck, the one who caused Him to die. He never did. Do you know what this Man called me? Ramona, my name. He *saw* me. He didn't see what I did wrong. He saw *me*. He died for *me*. He loves *me*. He volunteered His bloody and abused body to be nailed to a wooden Cross. His two hands and two feet were stabbed with nails to keep Him on that Cross. He was jabbed in His side with a spear. He was humiliated. There was no legal reason for Him to have died. But He did it out of choice...because He *loves* me.

He died, also knowing that I would one day love Him.

Jesus Christ, God clothed in flesh, came to Earth to serve as an eternal sacrifice for us. It's because of His death that I have the opportunity to spend forever in Heaven with Him. His Blood allowed me to escape spiritual death and eternal separation from God. His

Blood allows me to be healed and whole and enjoy my life on this planet. What a demonstration of love!

The account described is not an actual account (I obviously wasn't there for the crucifixion). It is, however, a mixture of how I would've responded had I been present. It also reflects how I have felt spiritually in my walk with Him.

He sees YOU! He calls YOU by name! He loves YOU! He did all of that for YOU!

Listen. I know that you've been hurt. I know that your heart has been broken. I know that life has hurt you terribly. I know. But there is a Man who loves you more than life. The same Man who got on a Cross and died for me, did the same for you. You were on His mind as He endured every beating on His way to the Cross. It is because of Him that we have hope. It is because of His blood that we have access to His Spirit that comforts and empowers us.

Jesus Christ is my Savior. He is the reason why I'm okay today. He's the reason why I've been able to heal and move on from so much hurt. He's the reason that I had a second chance at life. I shouldn't be here today. I shouldn't. But God ensured that, through Jesus, I had a way out.

His ending was bloody. It was brutal. It was so, so ugly. But it was *so* beautiful. His blood makes every ugly part of me so beautiful.

Scars. Bruises. Blood. Screams. Tears. Those things aren't pretty; but they tell my story. Call me ugly, if you must. But the ugliest things led me here; and I'm the most beautiful I've ever been. The same is true for you.

PRAYER

Now, it's your time to pray. Pray this prayer with me:

Lord, I confess with my mouth that Jesus is Lord and believe in my heart that God has raised Him from the dead, which allows me to be saved. Jesus came that I may have life, and have it more abundantly. The promises of God are "Yes" and "Amen." Everything that You have spoken over my life is true. Restore my faith. Help my unbelief. Help me to receive Your love. Though it is too wide or deep for me to fully comprehend, teach me about Your love for me. It is true. You love me with an everlasting love; with lovingkindness You draw me. As I draw near to You, You draw near to me. You've been waiting for me to respond to you. Now, I respond. I open the door and let You into my life. I need You. I love You because You first loved me. Nothing can separate me from Your love. Though I walk through the valley of the shadow of death, You are with me to comfort me. I am never alone because You will never leave or forsake me. You are a God who understands everything I've walked through. Because of that, I can approach You boldly with every need. I place my heart in Your hands. That's the safest place there is. I trust You. Jesus is my Savior. I will not go back. From this point on, I will walk forward with Your hand in mine. Thank You for being the ultimate sacrifice. In return, I sacrifice my pain to love You freely. I love You. Let's walk.

In Jesus' name, I pray. Amen.

APPLICATION

Get in an area by yourself. Listen to the below songs. Invite the Lord into your heart. Invite Him into your space. Let the songs speak to you. Rest in the presence of God. Be loved.

SONGS

"Worth" by Anthony Brown

"The Blood" by Naomi Raine featuring Dante Bowe

REFLECTION

CONCLUSION

We made it, y'all!

Thank you so much for purchasing and reading this book. This was a labor of love, birthed from a place of pain. Pain *always* produces purpose. ALWAYS. Every tear, sleepless night, stressor made way for this profound piece. God, thank You for getting this out of me. I am thankful for His patience with me. What felt like an unbearable breaking was really a collision with a promise. For years, people have confirmed that I was meant to write. It wasn't until I was almost 40 years old that the first book was written. Pain pushed me to start doing what I was called to do. It couldn't have happened before now. The timing is perfect. I'm so thankful. No matter who you are, where you are, or what you're going through, please know that there is purpose attached to you. It's never too late to pursue that.

This year, I made a promise to myself. I promised myself that I would LIVE this year. The last few years have been very difficult, and I was overcome by circumstances so many times. It was exhausting. Though I cannot control circumstances, I can control how they affect me. I decided that I was going to LIVE (and thrive) this year. No matter the situation, no matter who came, no matter who left, no matter the gain, no matter the loss…I was NOT going to be overtaken this year…for any reason. I decided to love myself the way I loved everyone else. Though I've had days to work through, I have kept that promise to myself. This book is proof of that. It is a testament of God's grace and personal perseverance.

This book is my baby. It was an unexpected surprise. Really, I had no idea I was going to write a book until a couple of days before I started writing it. I didn't know what it was going to be or when it would be finished. All I knew is that God wanted me to write; so I did. I'm thankful for His voice in my life. His voice revealed what was beautiful in me by exposing all of the ugly things. I expect that His voice will do the same for you.

Have I arrived? No. Do I have all of the answers? No. Are there still ugly pieces of me? Yes. I still have lots of work to do. I'll be in a process for the rest of my life. That's true for all of us. But I've learned a lot, and have grown so much! I'm thankful. Make sure you celebrate your growth. That's important.

In all of that, this book is not about me. This book is about you! It is *for* you. My tears were shed so that you wouldn't have to cry. I lost sleep so that you could gain rest. My story is to help save you years of trouble and propel you forward. Purpose is always about who you can help and serve. It is my greatest prayer that you are encouraged and hopeful. It is my heart's desire that you have unpacked all of the ugly things about your life and begun using them to polish the beautiful things about yourself. Be encouraged! There is hope! It's not too late! If I can overcome, you can too.

Decide to heal. Do the work. Commit to the process. You cannot avoid the process. But you are graced to walk through the process. You're worth the investment!

You are beautiful! That's not exclusive to the women reading my book. Men, every part of you is beautiful! You are special! There is no one else like you; and that's an advantage. Embrace that.

Don't quit! You can do this! We've got this!

I love you. I am praying for you.

xoxo,

Ramona

REFLECTION

RESOURCES

Therapy

Growth Therapy Center

Anita Stoudmire,

Licensed Professional Counselor and Coach

www.growththerapycenter.com

Instant Friend Service

Hey Giirl

Tameka L. Webb, Owner and Published Author

www.heygiirl.com

National Suicide Prevention Lifeline

800-273-TALK (8255)

Substance Abuse Mental Health Services (SAMHSA)

National Hotline

800-662-HELP (4357)

ABOUT THE AUTHOR

Ramona Ragland is a Richmond, VA native; an east coast girl. Family is a priority to her. She comes from a large family, who means the world to her. She also has an amazing set of friends that she adores.

She graduated from Virginia Commonwealth University (VCU) with a bachelor's degree in Business Management. She has been a professional in Corporate America for almost twenty years, serving as a trainer, content creator, mentor, auditor, among other things. Last year, she started her own business, as a writer for others. She is a Certified Master Trainer and has also received her Six Sigma Green Belt certification. Her passions include public speaking, people development and engagement, and process improvement.

Ramona is a licensed minister with years of church involvement. She loves people and serving them brings her joy! She has overseen multiple ministries and served as a Youth Pastor. A few years ago, she embarked on her first missions trip to Honduras to help children and families in a remote area. Connecting with people, singing, writing music, and praying are some of her favorite ways to serve. She is an out-of-the box leader who believes in meeting people where they are and loving them there.

Ms. Ragland is a simple girl, who enjoys laughing, dancing, and singing. She loves red lipstick and a mean pump. She enjoys the country, soaking up the sun, and listening to good music.

Connect with her on social media:

Instagram and Facebook: @ramona.josette

Website: www.ramonajosette.com

Post your story and pictures of your copy of the book, tag her, and use the hashtag #myuglybook.

www.ingramcontent.com/pod-product-compliance
Lightning Source LLC
Chambersburg PA
CBHW031400160426
43196CB00007B/839